BENNY
FLIES A NIGHT PASS

WRITTEN BY ANTHONY JUKER

ILLUSTRATED BY RITUAL

BENNY FLIES A NIGHT PASS

WRITTEN BY

ANTHONY JUKER

ILLUSTRATED BY RITUAL

For Mary, your endless encouragement is the lift for my wings.

Benny is a pilot! Benny likes to fly!
Benny shoots off the boat and into the sky.

Benny flies his departure today.
Up high, he watches the sun go away
with hope the moon will come out to play.

He checks his charts and to his demise,
only stars, a heavy heart, he wants to cry.

His friend says, "Don't worry, my dude. I got your back. We still got three hours til the Marshall stack."

They do their mission, flying circles in the sky. Benny counts the stars as they pass by.

As the time draws near, with darkness around, time to start thinking about coming down.

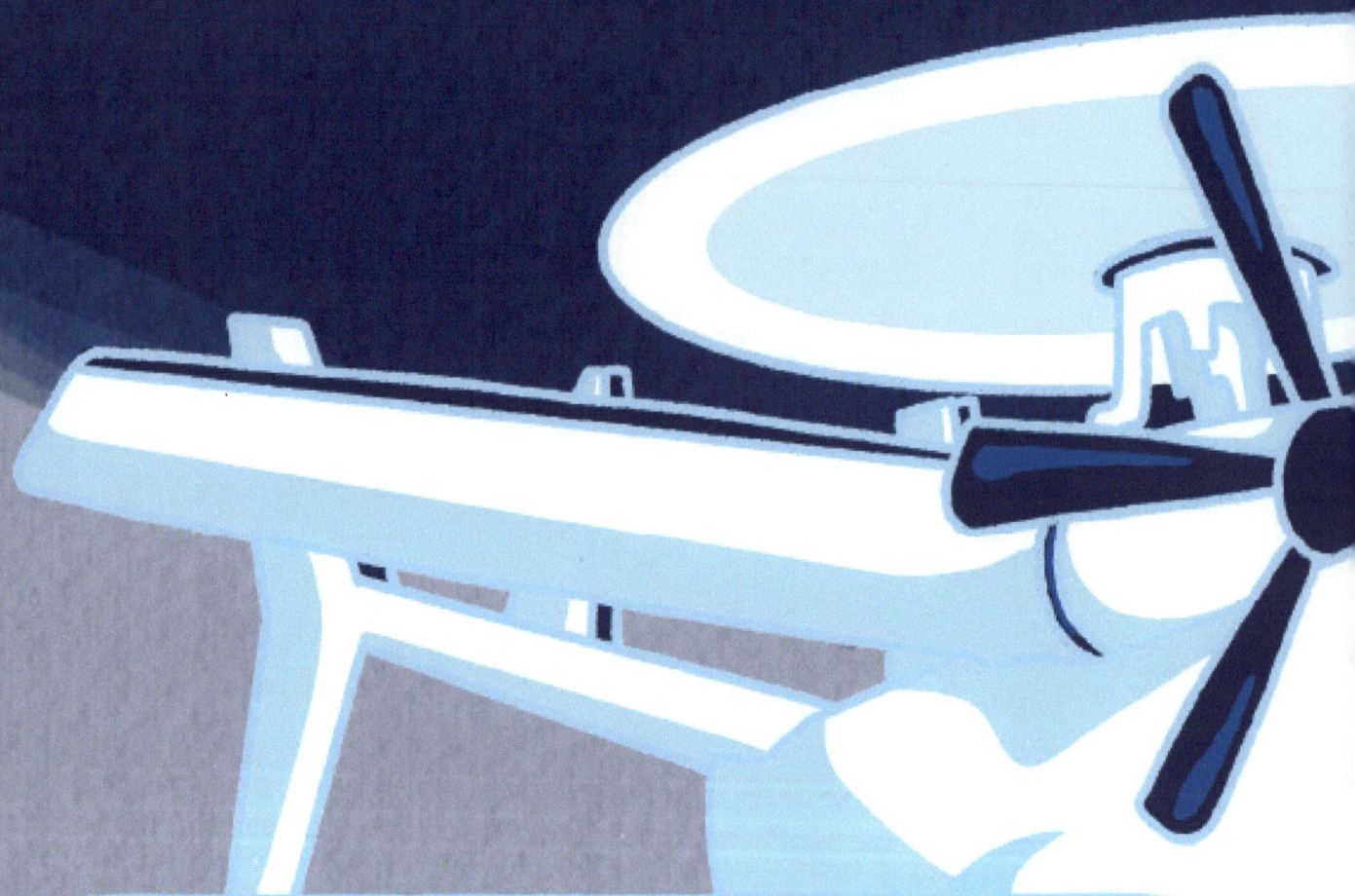

"Approach checks, please!" Benny commands.

SWEET SWEET!

Cries Marshall,
Red Crown and Strike.

Then with a steep climb
to the top of the stack
they hike.

"Established with gas!" Benny exclaims.
"Standby, wait, you're definitely last,"
Marshall explains.

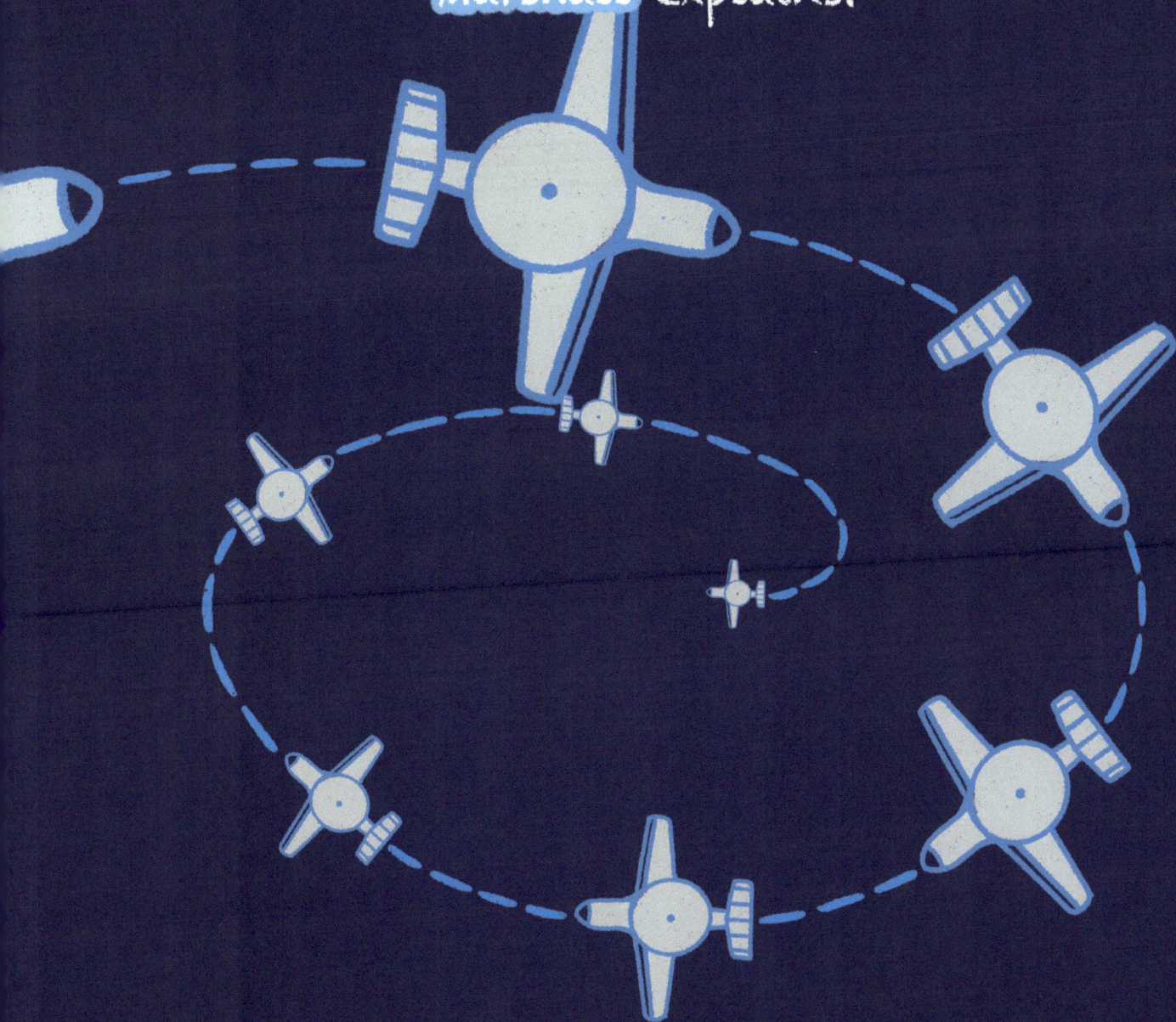

In circles they go, no end in sight.
It's one of the darker scarier nights.

Nervous and scared, he flies towards **mom**, a **white knuckle sleigh ride**, sweat covering his palms.

Down the chute Benny dives,
waiting for needles to come alive.

"I got the needles," Buddy utters.
"Fly up, fly right, will shoot us
right towards her."

"That's the speed. Let's dirty up. Gears,
flaps, and rudder, nothing's stuck."

Double-check me please, don't forget the **hook**! If we forget that, our goose is cooked.

With **glideslope** alive,
they come on down,
600 a minute
towards the ground.

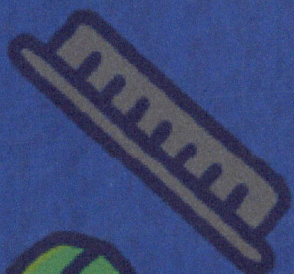

Falling out of the night,
the controls stiff and fickle,
Benny hopes his boy is on the
pickle.

There's the **boat**, just take a peek!
It looks like a **crester.** Benny has
great technique.

"I got a **ball,**" Benny declares. A slight
drift starts to build, Benny unaware.

"Call the ball when you got it,"
CATTC cries, the first thing they've said
all night that wasn't unwise.

"Little right!" says Paddles. Benny drops
the wing and gets a big ole settle.

By one, two, then three,
Benny moves the levers up with too much magnitude
and degree. Paddles says, "Don't climb!" But little they
know, power lever movement would be just for show.

Stuck back at **idle** the **levers** stay, the **ball** climbs to heaven up, up, and away.

It reaches the top but it's not gone, there's still hope!

Benny betting on the farthest side down the **LA**, his only prayer that he could stay

on that flight deck no go arounds, on **CAG's** face that'd put a frown.

The **ball** hangs right there at the top but all of a sudden, it begins to drop!

On **centerline** he lands, the **hook** grabs a **wire**, then still they stand!!!!

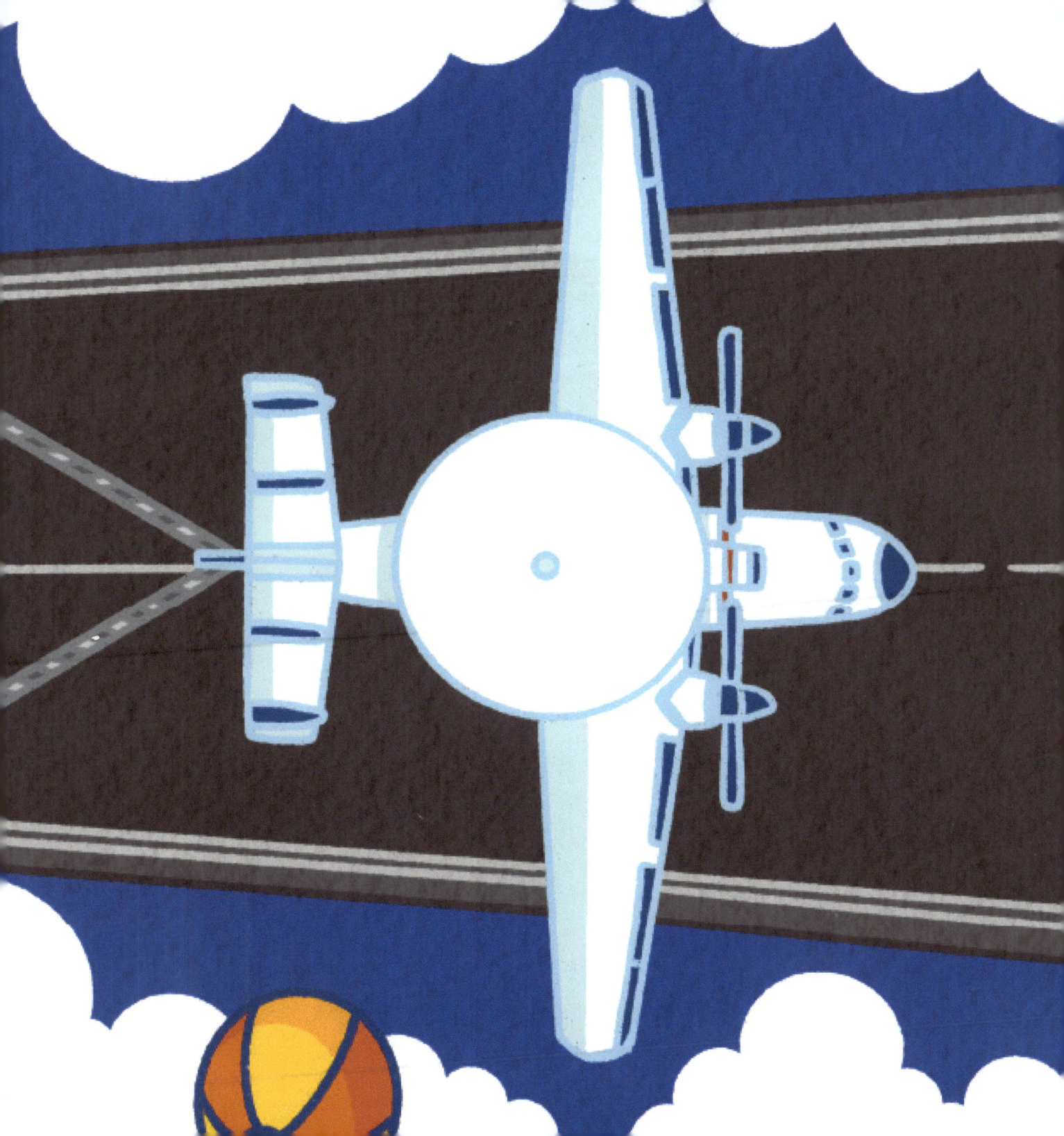

It was the last chance, the number four, a fair probably for Benny's score.

Hey, that's a safe pass or so they say, you'll live to fight another day. An oak next time or at least we'll see but for now, it's rats for ole Benny!

BENNY'S GLOSSARY

Boat — The aircraft carrier, a ship that holds 5000 people and over 100 planes!

A position behind the aircraft carrier where planes wait to be cleared to begin flying to the aircraft carrier — **Marshall Stack**

Paddles — Slang for Landing Signal Officer, a group of pilots that watch the planes approaching the landing area and talk to pilots to prevent an unsafe situation from developing. They are vital to the safety of the aircraft landing!

MC/Mission Commander — This aviator sits in the back looking for bad guys

A checklist that should be read and completed prior to the airplane returning to land on the aircraft carrier — **Approach Checks**

This is said over the radio when the aircraft carrier can see you on their screen — **Sweet Sweet**

Air-traffic controllers that direct planes around the aircraft carrier — **Marshall/Strike**

Red Crown — A smaller boat that protects the aircraft carrier

A term used over the radio asking someone to wait — "Standby"

"Make Best Speed" — Term used over the radio asking a plane to go as fast as possible

A slang term for the aircraft carrier — Mom

White Knuckle Sleigh Ride — Not a military term but it perfectly describes how tight someone might grip the yoke or power levers so hard the blood leaves their hands

"Chute" — Slang term for the path the plane flies, descending towards the aircraft carrier

"Needles" — A slang term for Automated Carrier Landing System (ACLS), these tell the pilot where the aircraft carrier is and what direction to fly

"Dirty Up" — A slang term used for configuring the aircraft to land. The landing gear is down and the flight surfaces are set to land!

Hook — Tailhook or arresting hook that catches the wires on the boat to land

Glideslope — The position in space vertically a pilot exists relative to the intended point of landing

600 a minute — Describes the descent rate or how quickly the plane is moving towards the surface In this instance 600 feet per minute!

"Crester" — It is the perfect place to be on glideslope, a pilot will swear they only ever see this...

Pickle — It is a stick that Paddles uses to control lights that have meaning to pilots

"Ball" — Slang for a light that tells you where you are on the glideslope

CATTC — (cat-see) Air traffic Control for the ship

Settle — When the aircraft sinks

Power! — Add power! You are low!

Idle — The lowest power setting possible

Levers — Power levers/throttle, the thing you move to get more or less thrust

LA — Slang for landing area, this is where the arresting wires exist and planes land!

Wire — Arresting wire, usually 4 exist, planes must catch one to stop!

Go Around/Bolter — When a pilot misses all the wires and must try again

CAG — (kag) stands for Commander Air Group, he's the boss!

Centerline — A line that runs up the very middle of the Landing Area

"The Number Four" — Slang for the last wire available in the landing area, usually a pilot's last hope!

"Oak" — Slang for "OK", the best grade a pilot can receive for an above average pass

Fair — A grade given to a pilot for an average pass

"Rats" — Slang for midnight rations, a meal occurring between 11pm and 2am where eggs are served and aviators recount their day together!

www.ingramcontent.com/pod-product-compliance
Lightning Source LLC
Chambersburg PA
CBHW041428090426
42741CB00002B/78